HEALING GRANTED

A Journey in Selflove

Shanie Ecole

Healing Granted by Shanie Ecole

Published by Healing Granted by Shanie Ecole

Spring Texas

No part of this book may be used or reproduced by any means, graphic, electronic, or mechanical, including photocopying, recording, taping, or by any information storage retrieval system without written permission of the publisher, except as provided by the United States of America copyright law.

Cover Artwork: Candace Katsaros

Text set in Garamond

Interior Photography: Trinity Thibodeaux: Used by permission

Copyright 2022 by Shanie Ecole

All rights reserved.

Library of Congress Control Number

2023907929

ISBN: 978-0-578-39859-4

First Edition

10 9 8 7 6 5 4 3 2 1

Printed in the United States

In loving memory of
Kalea Claire O'Callaghan
Sunlight Daydreamer

Acknowledgements

Butterflies', frogs' Sunshine, Dragons Anjels, Mystics and dragonflies oh my lol

The Universe is amazing! I am in total gratitude for this whole experience on so many levels I don't know where to start but to say THANK YOU!!!! Thank you!!! Thank you.

To my mini me(s) and Tee-Tee babies you inspire me to be better in every way… To love UNCONDITIONALLY, to be selfless and find balance in my care for you and myself. It's sometimes a thin line but my walk is purpose filled and even on the days I doubt myself you remind me not just who I am but how much I am loved.

Limitless!!!! This is for you… My ancestors say.

My soul tribe is vast and wide, and they are incredible… from being my sounding board to pushing me out of my comfort zone… they sincerely got my front back and sides pieces too lol. Thank you for being the mirror, applying pressure, helping create the breakthrough. Thank you for being available for those late-night visits early morning calls listening through Queenie voicing her opinion to crying through the frustration. My circle heals and it's not just a beautiful thing.

This is Iconix!

The hanging out with Gods and lunch dates with Goddesses full of empowering encouragement through love and "you got this."

There were historic photo shoots with dancing ballerinas. The comedy of getting me "straight" talks to feeling just right. The hugs and the pick me ups, the rose filled self-care days to my biggest fans …family was first). Love is permanently surrounding me overflowing in laughter and if a picture is worth a thousand words… lifetimes would pass and the memories would still be flowing, healing … pass the mic in vibrant hairstyles because love is ...

BFF(s), brothers, sisters, Queens, Kings

Loved Men Women my heartbeats.

My cup runneth over.

Tags to bolts and if I didn't tell you I love you today just wait because I will.

My loves thanks for believing in me.

Healing truly is Granted.

Rise

Dear My Beautiful Sunrays

Thank you for taking this journey with me and allowing me to be a part of yours. I was scared and nervous as I began writing this which made me feel uncomfortable at times, but I kept pushing. I started with setting boundaries with people, and truly loving on myself and making me a priority. Yes, self-love and self-care. I believe people deserve to be whole and like myself sometimes could use some encouragement. So, with so much love in my heart and divine guidance I began the process of healing by sharing out loud what we've been taught is taboo. I begin with journaling and meditating to finding my tribe which shifted everything. It wasn't the easiest task but there I was changing my life.

My hope is that by you knowing you are not alone you will find what you need to move forward abundantly and renewed. Each letter, each poem, affirmation, meditation and every gratitude is there to help you take your pieces back. You don't need anyone else's permission to heal. May this help you process your journey and begin to live your greatest life walking in your power.

With high Vibrations

I am sending you love, light and hugs

Shanie

> PS … you will need a journal for this journey….
> I left you space to start.

Table of Contents

Acknowledgements iv

Rise vi

You 1
   Letter to the Little One 2
   Letter to the Young One 3
   Letter to you Future self (you) 4
   Journal Space 5

She 7
   Letter to a Grandmother 8
   Letter to a Mom 9
   Letter to a Mama 11
   Letter to a Auntie 12
   Letter to a Daughter #1 13
   Letter to a Daughter #2 14
   Letter to a Daughter #3 15
   Letter to a Sissy 16
   Letter to a Young lady 18
   Letter to a Sister 19
   Letter to a Little Sister 20
   Journal Space 21

He 23
   Letter to a Grandfather 24
   Letter to a Dad 25
   Letter to a Daddy 26
   Letter to a Son 27
   Letter to a Brother #1 28
   Letter to a Brother #2 29
   Letter to a Young Man 30
   Letter to a Loved Man 31
   Journal Space 33

Them 35
   Letter to a Love #1 36

Letter to a Love #2	38
Letter to a Love #3	39
Letter to a Love #4	40
Letter to a Love #5	41
Letter to a Love #6	42
Letter to a Love #7	43
Letter to a Love #8	44
Letter to a Love #9	45
Letter to a Love #10	46
Letter to a Love #11	47
Letter to a Love #12	48
Letter to a Love #13	49
Letter to a Love #14	50
Letter to a Love #15	51
Letter to a Love #16	52
Letter to a Love #17 (Grief)	53
Letter to a Love #18	55
Letter to a Love #19	56
Letter to a Love #20	57
Letter to a Love #21	58
Letter to a Love #22	59
Letter to a Love #23	60
Journal Space	62

Divine Extensions 64

Letter to Creator (Poet, Artist, Creative)	65
Letter to a Kalea (Claire)	66
Letter to a Precious child	67
Letter to a Kindred spirit(sibling)	68
Letter to a Beautiful Child	69
Letter to a Bonus Child	70
Letter to a Love (fur babies)	71
Letter to a Child of Rainbow	72
Journal Space	74

Spokenword 76

Apology	77

Loved	78
Healing Now	79
Box	80
It's Been a Year	81
Found My Way Home	82
This Street	84
Reflections of Her Love	85
Faded	87
Thank You	88
Parts of Me	89
Time For a New Story	90
Farewell	92
Beautiful Goodbyes	93
I Am Woman	95
Beautiful Disaster	98
Hue Man	100
Trust	102
Rainwater	105
I Am Already Legendary	109
Healer of the Light	111
Charge It to My Head	114
Courage to Leave	117
Forgiveness	119
Healing Comes in Time	120
Why Can't You Love Me	121
I Know Love (Love Is….)	123
Affirmations	**126**
Affirmation 1	127
Affirmation 2	127
Affirmation 3	128
Affirmation 4	128
Affirmation 5	128
Affirmation 6	128
Affirmation 7	129
Affirmation 8	129
Affirmation 9	129

Affirmation 10 129
Affirmation 11 129
Affirmation 12 130
Affirmation 13 130
Affirmation 14 130
Affirmation 15 130
Affirmation 16 131
Affirmation 17 131
Affirmation 18 131
Affirmation 19 131
Affirmation 20 131
Affirmation 21 132
Affirmation 22 132
Affirmation 23 132
Affirmation 24 132
Affirmation 25 133
Affirmation 26 133
Affirmation 27 133

Meditations 134
Release Meditation 135
Unapologetic Meditation 136
Love Meditiation 137
The Secret Meditation 140
Powerful Person Meditation 141
Faith Meditation 142
Roots Meditation 144
Intense Day Shower Meditation 146
Gratitude Shower Meditation 147

Gratitude 148
Gratitude # 1 149
Gratitude # 2 149
Gratitude # 3 149
Gratitude # 4 149
Gratitude # 5 150
Gratitude # 6 150

Gratitude # 7	150
Gratitude # 8	150
Gratitude # 9	150
Gratitude # 10	150
Gratitude # 11	151
Gratitude # 12	151
Gratitude # 13	151
Vibe Check	152
Vibe Check Puzzle	153
Triumph	154
Dear My Sunray	155
About the Author	156
A word from the author	157

You

Time: **Date:** **Mood:**

Dear Little One,

You are the light of the world! You don't know it yet, but you are peace in the flesh, you are the vibration of joy, and you radiate kindness, and you are immeasurably loved. Your eyes carry messages in each twinkle...beautiful how they shine from the inside out. You are the very image of strength ...

You can see that in your eyes too. You are even stronger than you think. Speaking of thinking ...you are so intelligent. Your wisdom is unparalleled. You are wise far beyond your years and it's amazing. Your smile lights up a room and your laughter contagiously unmistakable. Your hugs are magic, and your kisses heal. Your spirit ... a breath of fresh air. There is a power in your words so always speak life... You are love and you are loved. So let your light shine brightly always.

Time: **Date:** **Mood:**

Dear Young One,

Embrace your journey.

Allow it to flow.

You're worth every breath it takes to get there.

And there is just the beginning…

There will be tears, laughter, joy but most importantly there will be you!

Healing Granted

Time: **Date:** **Mood:**

Dear Future self (you),

It's me

Breathe

Now look how far you have come... Thank you for continuing to get up.

I know being knocked down, mistreated and unappreciated was hard to bounce back from. You have been through more than any one person should and it is Beautiful how you rose to every occasion with such grace. Yesterday's challenges is said to be today's joy but the truth is yesterday was the lessons we had to learn to move forward it. And forward we went. Thank you it prepared us for greatness. Our growth was amazing. We learned the value of kindness not just to others but to ourselves. We learn to appreciate victory, especially the small ones.

They meant so much.

We discovered that not every storm was meant to disrupt us.

Some were cleansing.

While others a fresh start

We traveled many paths.

Not because we didn't know where we were going but for these are our connections and we made them.

We were never lost, we only needed to recognize who we were.

I love how when we truly embraced ourselves and all our perfect imperfections we began to truly elevate.

Loving ourselves we embraced peace and how very deserving we are and always have been. Thank you for allowing yourself... us to heal.

You are truly magnificent.

Healing Granted

Journal Space

Journal Space

She

Time: **Date:**   **Mood:**

Dear Grandmother,

Thank you for guiding me when I was lost.

For loving me when I thought I wasn't enough

For showing me how to get up. When I was bruised you reminded me, I wasn't broken. Thank you for the kindness you instilled in me. Your prayers gave me peace. Your love still keeps me.

I am so grateful for the amazing memories.

Did I tell you your kisses are healing... ha you probably already know that. While some doubt I am a believer. I am grateful for your words of wisdom, your hugs but most importantly how you show up for EVERYTHING.

You showed up for me.

And my cup is still overflowing with love.

Healing Granted

Time: **Date:**   **Mood:**

Dear Mom,

Today I gathered some old things and began gently unfolding them… they were fragile and worn. I found some had scratches and even holes where pieces were missing. There was a mirror that held a distorted image …one I didn't recognize anymore.

Along with many other things

I examined them thoroughly. Taking each item turned them inside out and right side up.

Making sure it wasn't something I needed to keep. I held on to them for so long. They were layered and scattered.

It was so much.

Many brought me tears.

So, I took the anger I had kept and folded it and placed it in the box. Then I took the sadness, and I patted it dry, and I placed it in the box. I took the hurt, misunderstanding and fear and shook it loose and it too went it the box.

I then took the unprotected and unsheltered pieces and wrapped them securely and placed them in the box. I looked around and there were only a few things left. I took a deep breath, and I exhaled as I picked up all the unwanted memories and all the things, I hadn't forgiven you for. I gathered the blame, dusted it off and put it in the box. I closed it, wrapped it in forgiveness and tied a bow with love and placed a tag of peace but rather than putting it back on the shelf I released it all.

Yesterday's memories are meant to disturb your present. They sculped you into who you are. Carrying all of those things weren't easy.

I had them tucked so tightly. You did the best you could. We don't have to carry it anymore. We are built from every mistake and mishap we learned from. We discovered how to release. How to breathe, accept gentleness and support. We learned about self-love, self-care and healthy communication.

Now joy is overflowing.

You see our purpose is greater.

Our love greater than all of those old things

I love you.

Healing Granted

Time: **Date:**   **Mood:**

Dear Mama,

I forgive you for all the things you will never apologize for…

It took me many years and I struggled. The needing for you to love me the way I thought a mother should but how could you…you may never know what that felt like… I searched for that in so many people always left empty handed and broken hearted… I struggled with communication, because we never talked… I was hushed left without a voice, and I imagine how you must have felt.

I struggled with being angry.

You were so mean to me like EVERYTHING was always my fault. Maybe you didn't know what to do or say.

I struggled with feeling protected… your absence left me vulnerable, but I took that and made it one of my greatest strengths. You see there is no handbook …simply lessons sometimes you don't get it right, but you keep trying. So, I kept trying no matter how much you hurt me or made me cry. The fight in me showed up in EVERYTHING I did … and when I got tired, I surrendered to the flow, realizing you would never apologize I would never hear "I'm sorry" so I forgave you anyway because I deserve more, and I won't carry that burden forward.

Healing Granted

Time: **Date:** **Mood:**

Dear Auntie,

Your love is sooooooo.

Healing Granted

Thank you for walking through life and loving me. I know sometimes it couldn't be easy, but you believed in me. Thank you for never giving up on me and not allowing me to give up on myself.

Your voice always sooth me. You reminded me that I was loved, and I want to tell you...your love changed my life.

I love you.

Healing Granted

Time: **Date:** **Mood:**

Dear Daughter #1,

Forgive me for not being the mother that you needed me to be… Kinder, softer more understanding…for struggling with communication. For the doubt and the fear that I may have carelessly instilled in you without thinking. For making you feel as if I didn't trust you to make good decisions. For making you feel as if you weren't good enough or that I didn't want you. For Being stuck in the past…sometimes even angry and taking it out on you only to realize it after I lashed out or not realizing it at all. For teaching you how to survive rather than how to live. For talking about being here but not being present to what you needed the most. Your love is far more powerful than any fear. I sometimes pushed you hard but it's only because I wanted to see you reach the stars…I wanted to see you successful even if it didn't look like it. I missed the fact you are already a thriving success because.

You show up every day.

In fact, I missed so much. How… you smile when you are sad and sometimes you cry when you are happy, but you refuse give up and that's amazing. You never needed my accolades but my wish for you is to know you deserve love and you are loved. Your love and passion for life Is so beautiful and even healing.

Yes, that's it!!!

P.S Healing Granted

Time: **Date:** **Mood:**

Dear Daughter #2,

Please forgive me for my absence in your life

I know you don't understand and it's even harder to explain so what I will say is I was there and no not as often as I could have been. I missed so much.

I wish I had made more of an effort to be present, rather than just birthdays or holidays.

I wish I had chosen to give more time. To be on the forefront instead of sitting in the background

My love for you is so much more than the effort I showed. The pictures were always beautiful, but I should have been there for it all... the daddy daughter dances, the games.

The graduations, the celebrations. But I wasn't, it didn't mean I loved you any less. I can't change the past, but my hope is that you can forgive me for who I was at that time in my life.

Inconsiderate, selfish and not very thoughtful

In my mind I was doing my part. In my heart you were fine ... I prayed you were. She made sure you were. Look at you...The little miracle... such a powerful gift.

The fight in you is proof the big things come in small packages. Your light is shining on the world, and I am thankful I get to see it.

Healing Granted

Time: **Date:**   **Mood:**

Dear Daughter #3,

Forgive me for not knowing how to tell.

For wanting to protect you

I cannot change who I was, and the truth is it made me who I would become.

And with it came my greatest gift… you

I am forever grateful.

I learned how to be selfless, how to nurture and most importantly how to love. How to give of myself without exception. I was never perfect but loving you gave me so many of my pieces back. My hope is that you are able to see with eyes of love and a heart wide open…without judgment.

You see the mirror still reflects you and all your glory as you grow and transition …something's are harder to process.

So be gentle with yourself and loved ones as they unfold.

Healing Granted

Time: **Date:**   **Mood:**

Dear Sissy,

Just in that moment you came into my life and changed my whole world. You have been through so much and yet you never cease to amaze me. Your gift to heal is supernatural. Fixing others crown

Picking them up when they've fallen down.

Oh, the joy in the Journeys shared.

You made everything look easy because of you I breathe easier.

I know sometimes you get tired still rising to every challenge.

I imagine that could be exhausting.

Sometimes battling in silence

I see you ...I wish you could see yourself through my eyes.

Because all of the praise you get is well deserved

All of the wisdom you share is heard and the path you cleared served a love filled purpose.

The days I don't feel worthy you remind me of light. Your ability to give insight and how you keep getting up often makes me cry, Your kindness, your strength, your passion, support, your trust, your determination your drive.

Your dedication, your grit, your grind your tenacity your persistence your love your light is consistent.

Radiance in motion and you have

You touched my soul.

You recharge me.

My cup is overflowing.

I am so beyond grateful for being able to share this time, this space, this lifetime with you.

I am so thankful for you loving me.

Sissy love is … so

Healing Granted

I love you dearly.

Time: **Date:** **Mood:**

Dear Young lady,

Forgive all of yourselves!
For whomever you needed to be to get through it.
The anger you carried for what seemed like lifetimes.
It's ok to cry.
How unprotected you felt.
I know it wasn't easy washing away the remnants
Of shatter innocence
Burning the debris
Of the hidden secrets you thought you had to keep ... wondering ... on the inside screaming
How could they not see?
Why you self-medicated
Attempting to validate the emotionless movement as if you weren't worth more.
The wreckage that you called life that spilled daily ... giving.
Disaster after disaster
Giving more
Chapter after chapter
Like falling broken brittle tree limbs...
The Judgment and
Shame
Release that shit.
Breathe in this moment.
Allowing the memories of yesterday's scars to mend
Allow the walls to fall, so you can see clearly again.
The love, the beauty, and the joy you have in you.
Now start living.

Healing Granted

Time: **Date:** **Mood:**

Dear Sister,

I know it's been hard.

Getting up after being knocked down time and time again.

I know you don't see it but every time you rise to the challenge...

your light shines a little brighter.

Bringing more of the good stuff

Imagine you are feeling a little low but trust that.

So many things had to change to prepare you for the amazing.

Moments that are shaping your world for the better

Your love, kindness and support have shifted others' lives just like what's about to happen for you. ... Trust the journey

Healing Granted

Time: **Date:** **Mood:**

Dear Little Sister

Forgive me for not being who you needed me to be to help you grow.

I made it hard for you. I made you feel unwanted and unloved.

I pushed you away.

And often left you when you needed me the most.

I can only imagine how hurt you must have been.

How hard it was to keep picking yourself up and dusting off all the crap I piled on you.

I treated you the way I felt the world was treating me.

The difference is you were stronger.

You had so much fight in you. Such resilience

I wish that I nurtured our relationship.

Nurtured you.

My hope is that you have found a way to forgive me in that I haven't done for myself.

I love you even if I don't say it.

I love you even if I struggle to show it.

May kindness and peace find its way into your heart when you think of me.

You deserve the peace.

Healing Granted

Journal Space

Journal Space

He

Time: **Date:** **Mood:**

Dear Grandfather,

You never allowed yourself to get to know me.

You missed out on so much, but I forgive you.

It taught me to have tough skin. I learned love has no beginning nor an ending...

it simply is. I turned out fine all the same.

Healing Granted

Time: **Date:** **Mood:**

Dear Dad,

I forgive you for your absence in my life. I won't say that I didn't struggle because I did.

I am not here to blame you for the things you didn't see or the fact I was too young to speak.

But I won every time I showed up and you didn't. I don't know what kept you away or why you never really bothered to call. And yet still here I am telling you I survived it all. You missed my first words, and first steps showed the pattern you'd take. There were many awards received that you've never seen the missed the donuts with dad and the games I had. I'd laugh just to hide discomfort especially when I was sad.

You see it took great resilience to become the amazing person I am today. I wanted to thank you for teaching me how to hurt... from it I found comfort in the love I was given. I learned to smile through the storm and dance in the rain. The pain that came from your absence... I learn to allow... it pushed me past what I thought knew and I released it...

P.S. Healing Granted

Time: **Date:**   **Mood:**

Dear Daddy,

Thank you for being my rock.

For loving me just the way I am

I imagine that could be difficult at times. You trying to guide me and me testing every nerve you have, and still you were patient. Sometimes a man of few words and yet there was so much strength in your silence. Your actions matched your words. You always showed up.

Never allowing me to shortchange myself by reminding me of my worth. Seeing what I couldn't see ...the divinity in me.

Healing Granted

Time: **Date:**   **Mood:**

Dear Son,

She knew every time you shortchanged them.

Didn't give your best.

When she got tired of yelling...begging

She smiled because she loved you but inside, she was still heartbroken. Always left picking up the pieces. You see she saw your priorities in action... cancellations and postponements.

Those babies always came first, and her babies barely seem to exist.

She thought to capture every precious moment she could. Memories for you to share, because one day they would want to know why you weren't there. I wonder if they will remember those empty conversations because as much as she shared with you about them, they seldom stayed in your forethought. She didn't ask for you to give them everything. She simply asked for you to show up the way you wanted me to show up.

Not following in my footsteps. Stereotypic Absence. She seemed to make magic happen, the way she nurtured, guided and raised them with such love. She wasn't alone but she wanted you. If only that had been mutual. Still, she kept giving you chances, opportunities...Thinking each time was different, the day she closed the door was the day she started living again.

Purposeful movements

She didn't ask for the world she already had it.

The joy in journey of how they still flourished.

Healing Granted

Time: **Date:** **Mood:**

Dear Brother #1,

It's time for you to get up and move. You have been afraid ...Complaisant even.

You are more than you give yourself credit for

You are not your past...

Relationship, job, or mistake. You are far greater. You are how you get up...you're the strides when it gets tough. You are the love you carry in your heart. You are your very dream; you just have start. Your word should carry weight and your actions have follow through.

Now get up and show them who you are, I believe in you.

Healing Granted

Time: **Date:**   **Mood:**

Dear Brother #2,

I see you… yes, I see you.

Moving and making changes through the most challenging times

It's going to be alright.

You are the difference.

I know sometimes you are tired of giving, trust your angels are listening. They are supporting you out there getting it. The great I AM

I see the God in you. The good you do even through the restless night. EVERYTHING is going to be Alright.

So, keep speaking life

Your persistence and dedication is elevating you to a whole height

I see you.

So, keep showing up.

Continue doing the right stuff...those mountains will be moved I want you to know your smile lights up a room your hugs heal wounds, and your Love is the glue. You are not invisible!

My love, I see you!

Healing Granted

Time: **Date:** **Mood:**

Dear Young Man,

I see you getting up and moving thru the doubts, the fears, moving.

Holding back your tears because" men aren't supposed to cry."

Grit and bare it.

Nothing held sacred but I see you unlearning the falsehoods that say this is manhood. Speaking your truth … releasing generational ring

The circle that has kept you believing abundance isn't yours.

I see you creating change...turning the page and reimagining what is possible. Giving hope, sharing love

Speaking life, I see you.

Eyes wide open

Cup running over.

Intentional shifts

Noticing all the beauty in the moment, feeling free

Realizing your dreams can be your reality.

Laughter filled days.

Joy filled nights.

Perfectly brought together as you share your gift of you with the world. Healing comes in so many forms and your smile is so

Healing Granted

Time: **Date:** **Mood:**

Dear Loved Man,

You are all that is strength, all that is love.

You got this.

It is amazing to see you and embracing the courage to be you powerfully in tune your imagination gives you unlimited possibilities to soar you need only open the door.

Allow yourself.

to be seen expressing yourself...clearly articulating statements that are reflecting of your journey ...traveling in directions uncommon to others charting your own path defining you in your own right I know loved man you're up for the task. So, get up and move get up and do something different than they expected of you to

Go ahead and change the game, make plans exchange the necessary conversations create versus and alternatives.

Don't give in when the road looks rough.

Your tribe is vast and wide rooting from all sides so know.

You're not alone.

We are here for you when you need someone to hold space.

Or to remind you to take your place, you are greatness....

Your prayers are heard.

What you need will be provided for

Make room for the flow of abundance.

Listen for the guidance...

Loved man your gentleness is a breath of fresh air, and your hugs are (powerful)

So, let's be fair.

Those strides you have made have shifted things into perspective.

And you decide who you want to be … this is your story.

So, sow the seeds that attract real connections.

Honor yourself and all generations

Stop underestimating yourself. You are valued.

Your presence is felt.

The struggles weren't meant to break you.

But to open your eyes

Notice what is revealed.

Loved man.

Your resilience is unmatched …showed them how to give back.

You deserve that pat on the back … keeping walking in your gratitude.

Loved man.

Healthy looks amazing on you.

Healing Granted

Journal Space

Journal Space

Them

Time: **Date:**   **Mood:**

Dear Love #1,

I want to know.

Are you tired yet?

Are you?

Tired of running in circles.... Playing kings and queens if jokers are wild ...hangman perspective?

Instead, you continue taking all you can get and leaving those that love you to drown in sorrow & you without regret leaving them feeling broken or battered better yet unworthy and still

Craving you while you move on to whomever is next while but leaving the door cracked... easy access. So, you never really leave… you just keep taking pieces while they are begging for peace. Losing sleep

There are so many memories.

Are you tired yet of feeding false hope?

Only to bring more tears

Are you tired yet?

When the shoe starts to fit the other foot, or the reflection starts to look distorted ...will continue view through damaged lenses. Will it come in color or is it black and white classic

Childhood memories of

Feeling of not being enough to make mommy happy or make daddy stay...unconsciously following in the footprints

Of the absence you felt

Leaving trails of tears...ex loves in your wake… wake...are you tired yet ready to be free?

Tired of hiding your inner royalty then set yourself free (of the generational curses or should I say programmed verses

Do you hear the sounds of change?

Can you feel the release?

The severed ties

Now

Allow yourself to be.

Allow yourself to breathe.

Allow yourself to shift.

Allow yourself to love.

Allow yourself to heal.

It's time indeed.

Healing Granted

Time: **Date:**   **Mood:**

Dear Love #2,

God whispered your name and at that moment I knew you were special. I didn't realize you would not only change my life, but you were going to change the world. Your love was so big that you loved in a way that most people only dream of being loved. I believe they call it UNCONDITIONAL! Loving each person …

For who they were…not who everyone thought them to be. It was beautiful to see and yet challenging for me because you gave of yourself in a way that drew people to you, I thought it meant it was less of you for me. I didn't want to share you with anyone else. You see I had dibs on your heart. I wanted all your time, all your love. I selfishly tried to hold you as tight as I could. Almost dimming your light …But your purpose was greater…your passion greater… your love greater. I didn't understand that then so

I took and I took…seldomly giving…I was always in need… trying to steal your attention… I was wrong… you were able to move on and I am thankful because of you I have grown.

And your light continues to shine. God continues to whisper your name and

Everything continues to shift.

Highlighting your footprint in the sands of time …reflecting blessings and favor

All deserved.

Healing Granted

Time: **Date:** **Mood:**

Dear Love #3,

I'm sorry that I wasn't able to be what you needed me to be.
Kinder, loving, more thoughtful.
It was never that I didn't love you because I did.
In my own selfish way
I know it must have seemed so one sided.
So unfair and so very lonely. It made me sad to know or to hear you cry. Especially because I was the cause. You'd give me chance after chance because you loved me in a way I never knew. I didn't deserve the kindness, support, love or the way you cared for me.

I imagine it must have been hard to do with all the pain I put you through. I loved you dearly I never knew just how much until I didn't have it anymore. You deserved the world and what a world it became when you gave yourself all the love, you'd been given away to those who failed to appreciate it.

You were always my peace I should have been yours.

Instead, I was your storm of chaos.

I wasn't meant to be a part of your future, but it was a gift knowing and having you in my life even if I didn't recognize it then.

You were always meant to light up the world so keep smiling.

Happiness looks amazing on you!

Healing Granted

Time: **Date:** **Mood:**

Dear Love #4,

The truth is…

Apologies don't undo the hurt or make a person feel safe again. It reminds them of how fragile it all really is… the still loving you.

The still wanting you.

The lack of understanding

How you could have allowed it to happen repeatedly

And yet the door was always open for you.

They wanted to be special.

They wanted to be the one.

And they were but not the way they imagined.

Oh, the pictures we paint.

Sometimes they sparkle but all that glitters isn't gold.

Funny how distorted our vision can be. Sometimes its bittersweet, but be

thankful for the closed doors, changed pace and altered paths that ultimately lead us exactly where we should be…

Healing Granted

Time: **Date:**   **Mood:**

Dear Love #5,

Maybe these feelings needed to come up…to get me out of this rut… this hole… this nothingness wondering if you will return… your return to loving me… loving us…. your return of kindness

Your return to caring… you returning to show up because today your actions finally matched your words.

Eye contact

A nod of forgiveness

Heartfelt tears

Fork in the road

Chosen paths.

Parted ways

New journeys

Purpose Filled life.

Adventurous joys

Growth is transformation.

Healing Granted

Time: **Date:** **Mood:**

Dear Love #6,

I wanted to hate you but that's not who I am.

So, I had to let you go to find me…

And the song played loudly.

Echoing and repeating almost screaming…

And so, it began the ending of a journey… one that left an impression so deep that I couldn't see clearly.

Lost in love and alone.

Attempting to keep the fire burning …Holding on… to the warm memories of yesterday until the day the chill of your selfishness hit me …our spark extinguished.

An avalanche of emotions fell quickly, and a broken heart buried … what happened to me.

My need for you blurred the vision and I couldn't sleep… I prayed for clarity…those tears I had to cry until there was nothing left… empty … and now all of the debris and clutter are faded memories of who we used to be. I had to lose you to find me… and when I released the love, I had for you the healing came easy.

Treasuring every movement, I moved forward.

allowing myself to love … yes just love… love without hesitation …. love without expectation …love freely … no exceptions.

Recognizing my significance…I carry EVERYTHING in me and it's a beautiful thing!

Healing Granted

Time: **Date:** **Mood:**

Dear Love #7,

I wanted to unlove you.

But that would be unloving myself.

You have been a part of me from the first time we connected and though we have been going through changes. Demanding attention never got us anywhere except hurt feelings and still longing for one another. Often asking do you love me.

The answer is always yes…. yes …yes!

Years pass still yes.

But you were never willing give EVERYTHING… always holding back.

You called me your peace …but you never chose me even still I breathe you in my dreams … you never loving yourself enough to heal so you damage those that love you…

Taken for granted feels like… the side effects of you.

Letting go…

The recovery sounds like healing

Oh yes.

Healing Granted

Time: **Date:** **Mood:**

Dear Love #8,

You said I miss you.

There was a time I believed it. Even a time I needed to hear it.

And I wondered what was it that you missed?

Curiosity got the better of me and I wondered if it was the sound of my voice that you missed...always speaking life into you. Checking to see if you were ok and letting you know you were needed too. Then I wondered if it was it my hugs maybe my kisses that made you feel loved or my scent... the way you used to inhale me. Maybe you carry it in your memory.

The connection we shared or the way we used to say we would always be there for one another .... time will always tell. Give you proof...evidence of the truth.

They were empty words. Adjectives not verbs. The truth is you aren't ready for the love you were given but you won't let go. The cycle I

Wanted to save you.

Be EVERYTHING you told me you were missing in your life.

I wanted to fill the void.

Our journey left me pouring all the love in you I could.

Seldomly leaving much for myself and you leaving me on "E."

I gave validation and comfort.

You gave satisfaction.

Leaving me in tears and you always missing me... the cycle and it ends here.

Loving me the way I always wanted you to love me.

Healing Granted

Time: **Date:** **Mood:**

Dear Love #9,

It sounded different to me... the closed door.

I quietly left... you heard it slam as it shut.

I understand you missing me and though I love you dearly it was past time to pull back my energy. Our exchanges were unequally balanced.

And the shortage left a void.

Much like you are feeling now. I never wanted to hurt you... those words echo so loudly at times.

At yet there were still missed moments filled with emotions, mixed messages and words that were heavily empty. Body cravings that made me believe that there was more to the time we once shared. Passion is such a funny thing... those memories have you holding on to bittersweet nothings.

Some lessons are harder learned.

Years of forgiveness and allowance.

As I stand in gratitude, I release the bond I once held sacred. Finally loving me more than I ever missed you ….

Healing Granted

Time: **Date:** **Mood:**

Dear Love #10,

I needed to cry.

I cried so much I became dehydrated with sensitivity.

Clearly

I can't eat the apologies or drink the

"I didn't mean too" you see...

I swallowed more... "I'm sorry" ... choked on more "forgive me" then I could count but I do.

What does you loving me mean to you...

One I am constant.

One is revolving.

And the common denominator you

Mathematically we match ...but there's the gap and it may take as many years to get there as it did to here ...life's a journey ...it's ok to ameliorate the trauma.

Healing Granted

Time: **Date:** **Mood:**

Dear Love #11,

There's nowhere to tuck this.

This weight of the world I have been carrying.

These mile high memories of yesterday.

There's nowhere to tuck marks left from your love.

Nowhere to tuck the tears cried while holding the ugly truth inside.

Nowhere to tuck the ache or the pain

Nowhere to tuck the generations of false truths

Nowhere to tuck the bitterness or the bitter taste

That residue that was choked on daily ... almost drowning... years of hiding the hurt years of stuffing it all away.

Years of pretending it didn't exist.

Those moments were stitched in memory.

Suppressed all the sorrow… ready to move on….

You not alone

Today you get to

Refuse to tuck anything. You exist.

You've been through some shit.

You refuse to quit.

You can now release it.

Give yourself permission to speak your truth!

Shifting into living out loud

Healing Granted

Time: **Date:**   **Mood:**

Dear Love #12,

Recalling things, you've said to me.

These after hour memories keep trying to disturb my peace but refuse to allow the past to dictate my future. I am thankful for every road I crossed, every door that closed but mostly for every window of opportunity that opened when I thought I missed EVERYTHING.

Gratitude

Because of where I been

I am here.

Because of who I was

I am here.

You wouldn't miss me.

If you chose differently

You wouldn't have to reach far,

But

You intentionally left empty bottles... smear makeup ...and ache in my heart.

But my darling

I've finally recovered from the scars you left.

The beautiful lessons I've learned…

…

Standing in Gratitude

And loved!

Healing Granted

Time: Date: Mood:

Dear Love #13,

Today I just wanted to hear your voice… I felt you thinking of me … you were calling to me intensely.

I wanted to answer but the truth is I am not missing anything. You are not who I fell in love with

Not the same person who used to love me.

Who I share treasured hearts.

I wanted to hear your voice … felt you calling to me and as many days as it takes, I will continue to cut those strings.

I love you but

I have enough memories.

I deserve to be happy!

Healing Granted

Time: **Date:** **Mood:**

Dear Love #14,

I heard music that brought tears to my eyes and for the first time ever I just let them flow.

My girl Corinna calls it the ugly cry.

It feels dead inside…

Mourning for so many reasons… you can't stay there. Awake to morning severed ties…dry eyes and a forward motion.

I've learned so much.

There are no problems, just opportunities to restart, recover, reshape and reinvent…

This chapter was called freedom and this the outro.

…Gratitude

Healing Granted

Time: **Date:**   **Mood:**

Dear Love #15,

There has always been a war of hearts.

I always chose you.

Bringing you out of the chaos

Even if only temporarily …

You said you wish you had more time.

You did but you only wanted the calm…

The peace …my love in doses

You chose.

I always wanted you.

But I no longer need you.

I have no desire to be anyone's afterthought.

… On anyone's back burner …I don't want to save you.

Though I have love for you

My heart calls and it no longer calls your name.

I am good with that, in fact it's such a beautiful thing.

Healing Granted

Time: **Date:** **Mood:**

Dear Love #16,

Don't drown yourself in sorrow. Our time together no matter how brief was nothing short of amazing. There were intense highs and challenging lows. But most importantly there was love. We shared joy, and laughter. We were the light and the change you wanted to see in the

world. So, no matter how you are feeling right now get up...

Get up and move. You can do this. Breathe you got this!

Healing Granted

Time: **Date:** **Mood:**

Dear Love #17 (Grief),

I wanted to call you.

I picked up the phone so many times...then I just cried ... like losing you again every time.

Pulling up to the house

But you aren't inside.

I heard someone say.

Life really can change in an instant ... now I get it.

We can blink and it could be over so how am I supposed to get over losing you. I can't sleep and when I do, I'm in search of you. Praying you show up in my dreams. I just want you close to me and I can't understand why you why now. You had so much more life to live and so much more love to give.

I feel like I am drowning without you... everything is moving in slow motion ...EVERYTHING.

It felt like the Heavens portrayed me taking you so suddenly. Grief ran so deep...I can't breathe.

And then one day I heard you whisper my name ... such a peaceful change.

Heard you say it's time again. Greet the morning with your love as you once did. Be open to love...to receive and to give ...you owe it to yourself to live again.

To laugh ...to remember joy and when you rise think of me. I stopped holding my breath.

It took some time.

To release all that I was carrying but today I got out of bed because of you.

Because you believed in me. Some days are easier than others and I allow it ...give myself permission to feel all the emotions...

I carry you in my spirit and

Your love still surrounds me for that I am forever grateful ...necessary connections.

Finally, grief and I have understanding.

Healing Granted

Time: **Date:**   **Mood:**

Dear Love #18,

I wonder…

Do they remember you standing in the room sharing poetry because the stage was where you were comfortable?

In your own skin

Where you didn't feel the need to fit in

Breaking down everything that stood in your way.

Those walls echoed loudly, and words nearly fell on deaf ears, but someone was there to hear.

Much like your time together ...muted tears

And a happy medium ...volume on it's complicated because your honesty was considered overrated.

You weathered years of ups and downs while they played with you like a yoyo…now you move against the grain.

Still, they won't let you go refusing until they are done claiming you to be the damaged goods. But whoa... how bright you stood without them there to dim your light standing grounded... releasing fight or flight.

vibrating voice of love

Intentionally aware

Speaking clearly

Notice the change in your frequency…

The world is your stage.

It's where you remember you and all your magic.

Healing Granted

Time: **Date:**   **Mood:**

Dear Love #19,

Thank you for sharing your energy in a way that is healing. Stepping with certainty like you were ready for anything. I don't know how you did it. You washed away those tear-stained watercolors filled with doubt.

Gently removing the deep buildup of "not enough " placing kindness in those cuts

You seem like you've been here before….

I watched you massage away the source of the trauma I held on so tightly to

Often showing me the mirror of the before and after. As the music began to change

There was a long release of pain that had been buried in my heart.

The days flowed into night and that trinkle of trust began to flow openly, some days I'm still in disbelief of how "did you get here". You were willing to dive deep… and I struggle to breathe, gasping as you helped me to let go of all the Doubt and fear replacing it with self-assurance reminding me to stand tall and as I did.

I felt rejuvenated.

And alive for the first time in so long

Understanding I only need to keep what's good for me.

The beautiful memories

Doesn't require repeating.

Lessons learn… letting go of the past and moving on.

Because I am worthy of this gift of happiness

I now Find myself in this place of gratitude I want to thank you.

Healing Granted

Time: **Date:** **Mood:**

Dear Love #20,

We didn't fail.

We learned what we didn't like.

What we wouldn't except

We learned what didn't feel good.

We came to understand what resonated and what didn't.

To me that's a win win.

Choosing not to stay where we are not happy.

Choosing to get up when we are knocked down.

Choosing to forgive when they don't apologize.

Is strength most don't understand.

But it's not for them to.

This is your journey, and you get to change the page and close the book.

When you are done

No one's permission needed.

Healing Granted

Time: **Date:** **Mood:**

Dear Love #21,

I want to apologize for teaching you how to love me wrong. For allowing you to come in and out of my life with all those "I'm sorry". For accepting less than I deserve. Calling the chaos love and believing that you could complete me. I made you responsible for my happiness. I tried to change you because I saw your potential. You see, we teach people how treat us by the way we treat ourselves and by the way we allow others to

I blamed you for it all. Forgive me for not recognizing it sooner.

The mirror… it's where we'll find it…the love we are in search of

UNCONDITIONALLY Yours

Healing Granted

Time: **Date:** **Mood:**

Dear Love #22,

In the beginning I wanted to help you see your potential. So, I loved on you as much as I could. I gave you what you seemed to be missing. In the process you became dependent ...losing yourself to the point of neither of us recognizing one another anymore. I believe we stayed because it was a familiar.

We kept rereading the same chapter but hadn't finished the book.

We were loving but only as far as we loved ourselves.

I felt the shortcomings. We were just existing, stumbling through the patterns… the habits we created. We deserve better.

So

I apologize for taking you through the shit storm and you are forgiven.

Letting go isn't always easy but we both deserve a fresh start, so I lovingly closed the book. Happy living

Healing Granted

Time: **Date:**   **Mood:**

Dear Love #23,

Imagine… imagine being with someone that ask GOD to help them love you correctly.

Can you see it?

As they help you unlearn the patterns of trauma you've had on repeat

Today they taught you how to cut those strings… now you are living lighter.

Can you feel it?

The weight of the world being lifted…such a beautiful gift.

The deep sensation of happiness

Flowing through you

Can you hear them rooting for you?

Cheering you on as you move with purpose.

Showing up has a whole new meaning they

Don't just support… they you understand you.

Someone that finds ways to make you smile.

Wants to hold your hand because your touch vibrates love.

So, cuddling feels like being reborn.

You become aware of how to hold space.

Share your thoughts, emotions and accomplishments.

Strides made in victory … here for EVERYTHING.

You match each other's energy …freedom to be who you were always meant to be…guided intuitively.

Everyday Motivation and what the Attention to details reveals is influential.

You know like the really small things.

Like good morning messages

Or asking how you are …and really wanting to know the answer.

So, are you ok?

Time for that

Needed embrace.

Can tell by the look on your face.

Moments like this you are present to because of everything you went thru prepared you for this.

You prayed for this.

Released EVERYTHING that wasn't meant.

You choose to break the cycle …no regret.

Love sacredly!

Yes, passionately loving intentionally!

Balanced with infinite possibilities!

Laughter fills the air.

What a beautiful vision

To receive

Inhaling the sweet scent

Of clarity

Healing Granted

Journal Space

Journal Space

Divine Extensions

Time: **Date:**   **Mood:**

Dear Creator (Poet, Artist, Creative)

With eyes wide open

I want you to know I see, I'm listening … yes, I hear you my heart wide open I feel you so please continue showing up. You speak life through your words, and though they are sometimes heavy you will be surprised how so many others needed to hear them to heal. Your courage to share is selfless …. Your colors form portraits paintings visions recognized even in our dreams …visions that resonate beauty and disaster through eyes of the many. Pushing them forward keeping them from being stuck in despair. Thank you for carving proof that you can work through it. Grow through it!

Reshaping this world

Styling these perfect imperfections

Creating laughter that shifts everything.

I know many days you laughed through your pain and as challenging as it was …you made a change… saved someone that day.

Your film was hard to see but necessary. Your works created victories like dominos released the strong hold …letting go …freeing up

Bringing us love

We are all connected.

And all deserving to be healthy so here's to showing up and shifting your whole world.

Healing Granted

Time: **Date:** **Mood:**

Dear Kalea (Claire),

You of many names

Healer friend sister

You changed my life.

The magic of you still surrounds me and I felt the loss as you returned home. I was overwhelmed with tears.

I unapologetically grieved your absence ...the truth that I also felt your peace. I can

hear your whispers of comfort. I know you are always with me. I am grateful for sharing this journey with you. My life is better because you were a part of it. You saw in me... what I didn't see in myself, and you nurtured it ... thank you.

Helping me to open up and be my authentic self. Allow my light to shine. Our connection is so powerfully beautiful. Thank you for your loving hugs, encouragement and all the love that you shared. I do miss seeing your smile... so I am so glad I have pictures...memories.

You are such a beautiful soul and I pray you had a peaceful journey as you returned to Great Spirit. Your healing light still shines brightly, dear one. Always you are loved and that is such a beautiful thing.

Healing Granted

Time: **Date:** **Mood:**

Dear Precious child,

Your love has always brought such joy in my life. Your smile is like sunshine. It brightened my every day. So, your absence is felt.

My heart ached ... a pain that I didn't think I wouldn't survive through. I felt you were gone too soon.

I thought I wasn't supposed to outlive you.

The grief felt almost unbearable. I couldn't breathe… how could you… my precious child be gone. Part of me felt like I was dying.

Getting up was hard but one day I did they say time heals all wounds, but the truth is love heals all wounds.

You see you changed my life. I was better because of what you gave me, what you taught me…who I became because of your love. My memories of you are precious and forever cherished. I am thankful you chose me. I can still see your smile hear your laughter and still feel your love, so you are always with me and for that I am forever grateful.

Healing Granted

Time: **Date:** **Mood:**

Dear Kindred spirit(sibling),

This might be a bit to process. I get it.

I know you don't really know me, but I want to get to know you... my sister, my brother, my kin.

I imagine how shocking this whole thing is and you are going through the stages of taking it all in.

The truth can be hard to handle but I am here.

Growing up in different households and finding out about you brought so many emotions, sometimes sad other times anger and although years have gone by, we still have time. We missed so much and even without them telling us the whole story... When you are ready, we can create a new one full of amazing memories. So, here's to us taking the first steps.

I love you already.

Healing Granted

Time: **Date:**   **Mood:**

Dear Beautiful Child,

I know it had to be hard moving what seemed like every time you turned around. Make a friend and you are moving again.

Truth is it was hard, but it made you who you are.

I know sometimes you felt lost, but your walk was designed to inspire the world. Everywhere you were ... supplied you with insight ...a different perspective.

Preparing you for your next step. Preparing you for all of this. I know it didn't seem like it, but the truth is that it's a beautiful gift. You became so aware that you seldom missed anything especially those details like discovering gratitude, kindness, forgiveness and standing your ground…

Wow look at you!

Standing in your power

So beautifully

No longer lonely

Just loved.

Healing Granted

Time:　　　　　　**Date:**　　　　　　**Mood:**

Dear Bonus Child,

This hasn't been easy for you. Some moments seemed awkward and others so natural.

Though biologically I am not yours… I am honored to be the bonus.

You see in my heart you always will be mine. Having you in my life changed mine for the better.

Watching you grow and thrive into the such a smart, amazing child has been more rewarding than I can ever express, and I love you more every day.

I know sometimes it's hard to place me…. Not sure where I fit sometimes.

Our exchange is one I am thankful for…the hugs, our conversations and the priceless memories I wouldn't change for the world.

Wherever you place me whether from a distance or close

You knowing I am here.

Is what's important and if you need me, I'm only a call away. I know you are strong and can make your own decisions.

I want you to know you aren't in this alone in this no matter the distance.

Over the years my love has only grown, and I am excited and proud to see who you are becoming.

You get to choose what that looks like

Healing Granted

Time: **Date:** **Mood:**

Dear Love (fur babies),

I heard.

Love has 4 paws.

You may be surprised to hear it, especially if you never experienced it yourself.

You see they radiate UNCONDITIONAL love.

It's amazing how they just want to be next to you. That brings them such peace that it pulls at your heart strings. Love me love me because I love you love you... they know when you are mad, they know when you are sad.

They are excited by your presence. They act out to get your attention.

And they wait patiently for your return when you leave. Protecting you from the wind, mailmen and plastic bags. Alert you to weather changes and they speak, and you understand and it's amazing.

They help you heal.

With love, kisses and cuddles

Every memory made is life changing.

Shifting you on your path

Defining love in a completely different way

Sometimes we struggle with their absence.

But that's when they show up the most...

Surrounding you in spirit

Always

Healing Granted

Time: **Date:** **Mood:**

Dear Child of Rainbow,

I see you,
To me you are sunshine,
Rocking colors of the divine.
I see you,
Trying to find you way,
Finding your words,
No more hiding,
Just openly being you!
The closet now only to hold fabulous.
clothes, out with old.
No longer looking for acceptance,
You are a blessing!
I see you,
Telling your truth,
Reminding them their judgement had
nothing to do with you.
Like who you like, love who you love.
I see you,
Letting go of the discomfort,
Finally walking in your confidence.
I see you,
No longer trying to blend in,
You understand you are born to stand out.
Live your best life,

Happy, free, and healed.
Shine your light brightly. Never stop growing.
I am grateful to see you embracing the harmony.
of your life. You are such a beautiful spirit.
Always remember who you are and that you are loved.

Healing Granted

Journal Space

Journal Space

Spokenword

Apology

I accept your apology

but you've been denied access to me

I will never say your love wasn't enough

But I will tell you I've had enough

Our love language is different

We have been speaking on two different frequencies and your vibration no longer vibes with me

And those memories we share when it was good are good but its go time or grow time

whatever the view it's fine

So I'm sending you love light and peace as I make my exit and set us free

Loved

Today I woke up grateful again for so many things
Grateful for you even with what we've been through
Grateful that I am able to forgive you
I realize it was harder to forgive myself
FOR the cycle
Each time we reconnected was another lesson
The journey seemed endless but so was our friendship
Never willing to quit
I was built different so
Every piece I recovered
another piece to the puzzle that was me
Trying to discover the big picture meant going deep
I often submerge myself even when I felt weak
Because love heals I had to believe
Because love heals I had to surrender and be willing to see
So I am grateful for each tear
Grateful for every year
Grateful for highs and lows
Grateful I've grown
So pardon me I shed a little light and I reassemble myself
completely LOVED

Healing Now

Sometimes …sometimes I wish that I could remove my heart
So I didn't have to feel pain
Sometimes I wish that I could remove my brain so I wouldn't think of you
Sometimes I just want to all go away
So will you go away…
Take it all with you
Leave no remnants
Take the tears
Faded memories
The wishful thoughts
The lack of balance
The needing of your touch
Because sometimes I simply just can't handle it
And I wonder if it's even worth it at all
It wasn't but I'm healing now ….

Box

.... Not meant to fit in your Box
I wasn't meant to fit in your Box

My vibe ain't like others
I love different
Every breath I take is intentional
My walks with purpose
I dance to my own beat
my tears cleansing
my laugh is unmistakable
my energy introduces me
there is a glow in my smile
A fire full of Passion in my eyes
I am my own kind of beautiful
if you've been loved by me your life will never be the same
growth is beautiful
I'm an amazing spirit wind earth fire and water
strength peace love light determination
I'm not meant to fit in your Box
I own my shh flaws and all
and I'm still amazing
I'm not that everyone's cup of tea
but I was never meant to be
I am exactly who I am supposed to be

It's Been a Year

It's many year since I heard the emotionless words fall from your lips
the same lips I used to kiss
since I shed tears until I became limp
I realize what we had wasn't shit
So I quit leaving you to live without me
without the friendship without it all
sometimes I hear songs and I reflect
bringing up those feelings I have to sit with
it's OK they don't mean shit
Hell I didn't
Yet you are forgiven
I hope that you found what you were looking for
no need to look at the door
I closed it behind me
Smiling at what amazing love I must be capable
to have loved the wrong person
through all of this stuff
to have continue to get up
how powerful it will be when the right person shows up for me

Found My Way Home

I'm not lost any more
healing comes in many forms
from forgiveness to self-love
my journey doesn't just look different ... it is
my path feels different because I finally gave in
I decided to take the long way home
venture to the edge of brokenness
walk where no footprints lay
discover the lows in the depths of my many missteps...
tear stained face
but I lived... you see
I've traveled in distant lands not meant for the fragile
touch things that only few people have touched
and learn the sacredness of my divinity while learning to forgive me
for the setups
row block after row black
leaving open doors and cracked windows tracking mud through my veins
calling it love
poisoning my heart first
then my brain self-inflicted wounds
doubting what I knew
but I'm grateful that I grew
severed karmic ties
cauterized with love and light

protection now placed over my life
yes the removal of all negative unbalanced energies
spirits and anything that's not for me
transmit all… covered in every corner of my life
prosperity flowing freely
abundance of healing
do you feel the peace
taste the love and inhale the laughter
hear the joy
yes I finally found my way back home to me

This Street

.... I can't be on this street

there's nothing here for me

except broken promises and empty words

so, I'm good

thanks for letting me know I crossed your mind I'm fine I know you reached out only to know with I still care I do but not enough to come back to you

you missing me is cool but I've been your fool

allowing you to continue to take

but that was my mistake and I pay my dues for loving you.

so I'm cool on you

I will always love you but finally… finally I love me more

There nothing left here for me so there's no need for me to be on the street

Reflections of Her Love

You said I love you… so with closed eyes open mind

I waited

And I waited

Many years I waited

To be over the idea of us

Didn't understand why you didn't see me as enough

I was there for you

I trusted you

supported you and loved you intensely

To the point I didn't recognize myself anymore

It wasn't until I realized

Us was never you and I

It was always you and she

Whomever she would be at the time

I struggled to get us out of my mind

Took so many tears …so many years

Letting go…letting you back

Ache after ache and break and break

But it's all clear now

I needed my beautiful seeds to be planted so the healing could begin

With eyes wide open

I see… I feel… I love

With intention and now that I let go and forgive

It's safe for me to live… my greatest life

I see the beauty

I see the peace
I see the strength
I see the healing
I see growth
I see her
Reflections of her love

Faded

The sound of disappointment was louder than yesterday's joy
the no call no show a mere reflection of a mouthful of lies
thankfully no tears left to cry
just an explosion of emotions until she becomes motionless
over the time over space where emptiness is always home
and yet taught
the difference between lonely and alone
they wonder what's wrong but it's nothing or it's everything
she said this thing you call us never had you in the equation
and every memory of him just faded

Thank You

Thank you thank you for reminding me how unimportant I really am to you

but I am very important make no mistake dear one

I have purpose

thank you for reminding me that I don't have a place in your life

Our Time is over

Thank you for reminding me that you will never love or care about me the way I have you

I have given away so many precious years to you

Lessons and blessings

Thank you for continuously breaking my heart over and over

so, I know that it can be healed ...I see the light in the darkest times

sadly, you say you hope I know how much you love and miss me

you show me by your absence ...today was amazing because with each teardrop

I took a piece to me back so thank you for showing me the way

Parts of Me

Parts of me still longs for you

the you that I fell in love with

the part that I believe loved me fiercely

The part of you that sent for me because you couldn't be without me

You know the part that would never leave without seeing me

When the calls were frequent and full of promise you know that part

I still remember but what if what if all the love I gave away was meant for me

what if what if what I was feeling was for me

What if I just poured all that amazing love right back into myself

how magic that would be

Time For a New Story

It's time for new story

He said I love you always

she believed him

But it wasn't enough to keep her holding on like before

The last letter was written.

She was giving in with forgiveness

I miss her

Well her is who you left

But I digress

Recalling intimate moments tears anger fear

Crossroads brought us here

She said I used to think if you love something you set it free

If it comes back then it was yours

But the truth is they come back because you didn't close the door

It felt good but it hurts

Its sounds good but it's broke

It looks good but it's not yours

Never meant to be

This doesn't work

It's time for a new story

Because love …love doesn't look like smeared make up and broken hearts

It doesn't look like wasted time

empty bottles of wine filled with "I'm sorry"

Or

Deep conversations full of plans that never come
But they are the one
Your choice makes you question
Because my love stays on your mind
But I'm fine
They can have you and you can have them
Sending happy vibes because now …now I can move on with my life
Removing what no longer serves me so
Making Room for the good stuff
No more wasted time
no more what if
I no longer dream of you
No longer craving to see you
I gave all the love that I could spare without becoming empty
So thank you for showing me how strong I really AM
And weak I needed to become
So that I could truly see me
It's time for new story
one that starts with self-love and vibrate so purely
so open so deep so healing that my heart speaks clearly
for everyone to see and it says I AM love… I AM loved
the forgiveness was for me
yes the forgiveness was for me
and now I can say I truly love you because now I'm free

Farewell

Can I tell you a story
One that whispers love so loudly
You felt it in your very spirit
The air you breathed sounded like healing
Laughing until it was contagious
Joy that is ageless
Our time never taken for granted
Wondrous memories to forever carry
Seeing it in your smile ...an outpour of love to go around
Resilient without even trying
Each step purposely guided
We are Divinely born
We are whole complete and Filled with Love
Simply transitioning
To more of the good stuff
Helping hands... trust of friends...family lineage that seems endless
Living without regret instead loving with intent
Yes being present...cherishing each day you arise remembering it is still a gift
Hugs are purposeful movements
Life is lessons and blessing.
Be grateful for it all
They say we don't know the time or the date and we don't
So start living
Forgive quickly laughing often and loving each other whole
Because that's what matters most... so wipe those tears find the peace in knowing my love is still here always with you even now

Beautiful Goodbyes

Beautiful goodbyes heard your very last lie
No more tears to cry
We moved on with our lives
Beautiful goodbyes

Too long have I accepted wasted time
I wish I could say you were out of my mind but every time
I look at her and she smiles I see you in her eyes.
And I don't regret a moment of her life not even the restless nights
You and I were tight
I saw change coming her way
I still remember the date
The many disappointments that followed
You missed her first words …her first steps
Its ok
It showed the pattern you'd take
By then you had already missed 270 out of 274 beautiful days of her life
Birthdays came and went
Not even a card sent
She doesn't remember your scent
And as she grew I never told her you wasn't shhh
Never blamed you for the split
I told her baby sometimes people are taking away from us
And we just have to adjust

So she learns to be tough
Intelligent confident and so much more
Showed her how when she is done with someone
Simply close the door
And when we fall how to get up
Because it is we that teach people how to treat us
Taught her the difference between love and lust
To know when and when not to trust
And how things aren't always what they seem
How to lead but follow her dreams
How to hold her head up so she can see what she's walking into
How to hold it up higher
Higher
Because the sky really is the limit for
Her
These are the things you never knew
The things you missed
These are her beautiful beginnings
And our beautiful goodbyes

Beautiful goodbyes
Heard your very last lie
No more tears to cry
We moved on with our life beautiful goodbyes
Goodbye

I Am Woman

I am woman

I am more than a pretty face

More than my shape

I'm classy

So more than what you see through your tinted shades

I am the sparkle in your eyes like bling bling

Yes there is more to me

Stillness movement

Sacred … Divine

I gave birth to creation

Bringing forth the light

Of humanity … here comes a star shining brightly …priceless

Yes, I am woman

So describe me in the words of greatness

They say its levels to this… but the truth is we are limitless

Not defined by your opinions thoughts or demands

Queens in our own right

Wearing confidence in our eyes

Fierceness In our smiles

Crowns of faith

Warriors living out loud

We have our own style

There is a softness that speaks …can you hear me

I am love

Strength that cannot be undone

My walk is with purpose

Who I am deserves be heard
Independent and determined
I am the Backbone and I know it
I am woman
Visualize it
We are the colors of the rainbow
Amazing and brilliant
I am woman
A force of nature
Natural unpredictable
Bold and ambitious
I'm balanced so my peace within is sexy
Reflecting the Heavens
We are contrasting in sizes heartfelt alignments
Yes resilient without even trying
Courageous forgiving enlightened patient
I am woman
Echoes of songs in my spirit
My voice moves mountains
Planting seeds
Creating my own reality
I don't need you to validate me
I have a Right to choose
Baby I'm I am nobody's fool
Yes I am sassy here breaking boundaries
I am woman
So here's to us

And here's to self-love
I am evolution amplified breathing passion into your soul
It's not where we've been its
Where we are going
I am woman divinely made
Now you know
Ladies let's go

Beautiful Disaster

Granted such a beautiful disaster
the brushstrokes of her paintbrush were saturated with lines intersecting with kindness and chaos
her colors deep vibrant and intentional
her setbacks remind me of tear-stained watercolors...
pain never looked so beautiful
aged by years of being a dreamer
abused by days gone by and still a never dimming light
you see her love was magic
rising every time she fell
she was free spirited and hell fire
More powerful than she ever could had imagined
her walls of protection as fragile as the peace she craved
and her adventures sometimes wreak havoc on her body
and the broken mirror a distorted image of life lessons
such a beautiful disaster
the misdirection merely the wings of change ...
you see when she got centered
The dust settled and EVERYTHING shifted
Almost like breathing life for the first time
Crayon scented Trauma separated by degrees of tranquility
because she chooses not to be stuck there
While life continues offer clarity through open windows and closed doors
her search for love resulted in loving others nearly whole ...
she often lost pieces of herself far more than she cared to admit
We sometimes carry other people's shit
Their judgment harsh and yet no one more cruel than she

A master at tearing herself down while building up those she loved
The listener the comforter the supporter
Forgetting that she too was worthy…
to be seen worthy to heard and deserving to be loved
Such a beautiful disaster
Her oil smeared travels took her far and wide her recovery sometimes slow
Sometimes like she was just along for the ride
Until she chooses to go deep
Willing to shift the energy
Doing the work and discovered
The love she'd been searching for was in she
Yeeess her own divinity
As she shed her shit layer by layer
Tear by tear washing away the buildup of the shit storms
She used to be so comfortable in
Removing her finger off the self-destruct …
finally embracing self-love…
releasing those memories and those stories she told herself
No longer the glue that keeps
Her inner goddess locked away
Her journey was sculpted by highs and lows
Molded by adversity laughter joy and resilience …
little did she know her footprint a pathway for others
You see the amazing woman that she had become
is because of beautiful disaster that she was
and she called this
masterpiece healing

Hue Man

King Brother Father son friend

I know it's been a while since you heard it…

maybe felt like you deserve it

Yes you

I want to remind you who you are…

I know sometimes you get lost

I sensed trying to find your path and at last

you radiate ***Shades of greatness***

Determined to make it

Challenges arise but I see the fire in your eyes

That smile that says this is my time

And I felt it

Some say stop looking back but I say look how far you have come

Creating legacies making memories

Inspiring many generations to come

Just when they thought you were done

You intentionally manifest love in a way that it becomes custom

As you humbly and confidently shine your light

Visions become clear

Providing protection and insight

I honor your tears

Your strength

Your compassion

As you strive for balance in your gratitude

I see the god in you
Royal bloodline of the most high
Sowing seeds of perspective
Purposeful steps
And I see the increase
Self-validation
A Comrade but never afraid to lead
Still gentle and kindness he breathes
Aware of the chaos but chooses his peace
Tasting freedom abundantly
His Roots go so deep
That his growth ...his glow up is on high beam
hues intensely reflecting victory …
and it's my honor to love and celebrate you daily 💚

Trust

She said I don't trust you
You play carelessly with my heart
Pulling at my heart strings vigorously
Taunting my emotions with love forever
Weathered storms and promises of protection
I don't trust you
You tell me it was love at first sight
Ask me where I been all your life
Tell me you would do life if it's what it takes
I'm your baby
You leave your hugs on my spirit
Your touch sown in my skin
And when I look at you
You look lost to your memories …mesmerized
As if you have loved me for lifetimes
I don't trust you
You pull me close and push me away
Sometimes keeping me at arm's length
Sometimes you take more then you give
And when I feel like I am at wits end
I hear sincerity and truth
I hear you say it
Don't you know you are my everything
I love you
You are my rock
And time seems to stop

I don't trust you
You say you miss right after I leave
And if all you get is 5 minutes it alright
Because you got to be next to me
And when you are next to me
You inhale me as if you found heaven's scent
I don't trust you
So every day I struggle
Whether to believe
When we are not on the same page
I don't wonder is it me
I wonder if it is meant to be
Because when you shutdown it frustrates me
On levels I can't explain
And I can't explain how your love courses thru my veins
And how when I want you my body aches
How your kisses make everything ok
I don't trust you
I wonder how you find my smile thru my tears
How I always wish you were here
Right now I wish you were here
You have a way with words
Sometimes you get on my nerves
But when you seem broke I want to fix you
You say you need me
Your glue
I don't trust you

As far I could throw you
So scared… scared because the truth is I love you
We are so connected
It feels like we are destined
Now we have time invested
I'm not sure if you are heaven sent
But when I inhale your scent
I become weak
You say you got me
I don't trust you
But You knew
You said meeting me changed your life
So You played with my heart vigorously
Repairing pieces of it daily
Tying love knots made pure as praline candy
Solid and sweet
Still unsure but you make feel so full
And as I reflect on time passed
Reflect on things and people that didn't last
I believe you were different
Because When I am alone with you
I feel at home with you
I feel safe with you
What if I just trust I am supposed to be with you

Rainwater

I walked through the rainwater
I felt the grass between my toes
I felt the earth feed my soul
I left fear in the past and I let go
Release relinquish let go of what was holding me back
And each drop cleansing
Removed the debris and all that stained me
Reclaiming a piece of me with each step
I found my voice in the rainwater soak and wet
The silence is over
Restoration at its finest
Because my heart wasn't broken
My mind was just clouded
Given pieces of me that wasn't deserved
Given trust that wasn't earned
I tried to love you whole because that's who I was
I wanted you to know true love
But
You got caught up
You wanted me to believe you but you lied
You wanted me to help you and I tried
But you made me shed tears I didn't need to cry
You made feel lost because you lied
But
I'm fine
Strong enough to fall and rise

Now

Smile because they say blood is thicker water

But pardon me as I splash water on that statement with cold truth

When you true

Real recognize real

So I forgive you so I can move forward

But promise I'll never forget

The look on his face when he had to tell me that shit

Thank you for blaming me

For telling all the secrets you promised to keep

For showing me who you are

Caring about no one but yourself

Yeah that representative is long gone

You know cards give confirmation

Yup that six sense is amazing

My love was never wavering

But now I'm focused

Changed

I'm destined because I'm already great

My prayer for you is that it's not too late

For you to get it together

Hoping that the seeds I planted can grow

They say what you weep

You sow

I been told you get that back 10-fold but I don't know

So

I walk through the rainwater

I felt the wet grass between my toes
I felt the earth feed my soul
I left fear in the past and I let go of your hand
Moving forward raised expectations.
With even more determination
I got places to go
I hate you ain't with me though
I was so sure you were the one
I was so sure I was done searching
I was so sure I was done hurting
But the proof was in the praline candy that I ate
It was a sweet dream
But I woke up and I've had enough
I learned if the feelings are mutual
Then the efforts will be equal
So I have to love you from a distance
I don't need you to validate my existence
Missing each other doesn't change it
We can't go back
That rippled effect
It's a lot to digest
So
I walk through rainwater
I felt the wet grass between my toes I felt the earth feed my soul
Left fear in the past and I let go
I lost so much
But I ain't sorry though

I'm grounded and happy to be me
With the freedom to just be
I know you didn't know the cracks let in the light
And the rainwater well it restores me to life
Loving
Born royalty earth angel healer and free
Never defeated
The rainwater restores me
I am living my best life
Smiling laughing shining brightly
Whole healthy
And you just get to miss me

I Am Already Legendary

I am the essence flowing through the veins of men
And when they hear me speak their hearts begin pumping at usual speeds
Excitement and peace
Direct connection to the Almighty
Your ancestors told stories of me
This generation says my poetry is on Fleek
And the conscious our future well they already know about me
I'm healing through these words so I'll speak volumes
Raising vibrations so do I have your attention
I've traveled to different planes …Other realms
Distant galaxies most can't believe
Just to remind you how amazing you be
I AM already legendary
I AM here to build bridges and break boundaries
Teach you how to manifest dreams …Teach you lessons in the truth
How to be still and make moves
Yes I believe in you ….
So I walk with the spirit of the sun
Released all negativity so here I come
Brace yourself…breathe deep
Some find it difficult to see
So feel me…fear free
Because what's for you is for you

And what's for me is for me

We crossed paths because I am a part of your destiny

I gave birth to creation so STAND UP AND WALK IN YOUR SALVATION

I AM EVOLUTION ON STEROIDS …breathing life into your SOUL

Yes your higher self already knows

So let me fix your CROWN… did you hear that sound …

You are ELEVATING NOW

Third eye open …I'll heal their throat chakras so they can quit choking…

Done

Words spoken …they said I was broken …naw I AM healing and growing

Pain is attention getting not a sign of weakness …I AM elated

Everything about us says we are already great

We got this…you got this … you better believe I got this

Cause baby I AM already LEGENDARY

Healer of the Light

Healer the light I used to cry at night wondering why me
until I woke up one day and realized why me
I understood the message
the 1 they spoke in silence but I'll speak
they tried blind me but the 3rd eye still see
thought that I'd be angry but I found peace
I realized that that doesn't weaken me
this is my destiny
I was made to heal so I had to start with me
and it doesn't matter whether you believe in me and or not
their doubts aren't my concerns
those obstacles I've removed
and those mountains you thought that I should carry
I climbed and what their view came focus
oh I noticed when you became nervous
I felt that shift heard the unlocking of my gifts
that click click clicking of release locks unlocked doors
yes I meant for more
the fire within me
burns away your untruth
your 3-dimensional mindful dreams ain't got nothing on me
they wanted me to stay in hibernation
but I felt the change in vibration
so you know you noticed the change in me
as I rose up because I'm not built to stay down

so you can keep your mind manipulation those lies and those half truth

trust me when I tell you that I see you

and you can't take away my right to choose

so you …you can keep your 40% and you… you can keep your government

I am awake from that slumber

a free thinker encourager and yes I am a believer

I am a healer and I challenge you to hear the silence in the noise

the misdirection and know you want more because I can feel your void

and you wonder why your all aura so dark and dingy that's that negative

and you ain't ready for me

I'm connected with heaven rings rocking my angel wings

Direct connection with the Universe

this lifetime so I won't wait

They say time is an illusion so no need to hesitate

just connect to my dots

and know their love is all there is

and yes my mission is just that BIG

and my seeds are 10 million times more powerful than me

so I have to nourish my fruit and feed them the truth

with love and guidance

and remind them that we are healers

so when they wonder who I am

and they're trying to figure out where I come from

can tell them that I am a powerful being
leaving lasting impressions
while balancing in these
I am a bringer of the water a drummer of nourishment
and it will be evident who I am
who I be
the sunshine still shining brightly
you can call me Shanie
some call me goddess
others call me Queen
my friends call me a blessing
and my babies called me mommy
Mother Earth calls me her perfect imperfection
God...the universe calls me his **everything**
but you might know it as the source of his reflection
I am a divine healer of the light
so there's no way you can block my shine
so there's no use of you even trying
so stop trying to deny who I am

Charge It to My Head

I did something I don't normally do
In my alone time I crossed the line and gave up
and it doesn't matter if you believe it or not
love me or not
Need me or not
This had stop ...beginning to suffocate
You stopped breathing life into me
And as a result I felt slower heartbeat
Became reckless emotionless
emotional as less and less time and air comes in and you want to come in
I can't breathe in here
you know the space you left vacate
Where you didn't want to be anymore
Don't take this wrong charge it to my head not my heart
I forgot how to inhale the sunlight that used to be your smile
Dimples on pow like laugh out loud
now that smile upside
I forgot how to hold the warmth that came with that laugh
we used to be having a blast thought
I found true love at last
I forgot how to let it settle so it could sink in
held you close enough too always hear our happy
so happy we were on high
Can you hear it
naw you can't hear it
You passing on spending time
Exhaling causing exhaustion
Because you didn't care

Slow… slow… slow down
Mind going a million miles a minute
Trying not to over think it
Trying not to over speak it
But we in deep or at least for me
Charge it to my head and not my heart
As if one has to do with the other ...
Trust It
for a minute it's going to be rough
In a second you will hear the crunch
Of your feelings as they crush everything you believing
one minute you cheesing
And now you disagreeing
You missing me more back then
Ain't got time
Fading shine
On that grind
Let's play rewind
Take a look when you erased the smile
Removing the pieces repeatedly
Messing up and I fell back
I was supposed to be your everything
Your forever, soul mate, match made in heaven but you selfish
The more I think about it...had to be a trap
so in love cause I didn't catch that
Love at first sight or love at first lie
Everything I saw was not what it seemed
Spare me anymore lies
I have No tears to cry

Because I am numb inside
Charge it to my head not my heart
I served my time and you served your purpose
reminding me that spots don't change
seasons do
With each season comes healing too
I am freed of the burden of wanting you
and the forgiveness ...
well I deserve peace not to be in pieces
So I released you
So here's to closing the door
Here's to loving me even more
Here's to spreading my wings and soaring
Higher than I ever could have got with you
shining brighter but you didn't have a clue
I am light blazing
No limitations
Afraid of my love because true love was something you never knew
But I am grateful for the lesson
Grateful because being able to love after loss is blessing
My destiny didn't lie in hands
So if it seems like I don't care
charge it to my head and my heart
Time for a new start
Now you know walking away really is an art
And this Masterpiece yup is called closure

Courage to Leave

I am screaming inside ...
now your trust is denied
Your mistakes don't define you
But they affected me... negatively
Your wants and needs are valid but mine are too
You are important but I am too
More than just a hashtag #IAMTOO
When trust leaves it's gone
And trying to hold on is point less
Point made trust me when I say I heard everything you said
And what you didn't say
We've come a long way
Much has changed and so much stayed the same but this our life ...
not game
You have crossed boundaries with disrespect
and there are things I can't forget
and there are things I refuse to accept
So I say no
No to allowing you to continue this journey with me ...
years don't equal loyalty
No to Holding on to those memories
Good or bad they are over now
No… to trying to save you...
you never needed to be saved…
just a clear path to walkway

No to being last on your list...
if you wanted to be there you would have been
You chose
I forgave you because you knew
We don't need each and yet you refuse to let go
Go: Define as moving from one place to another
And another is waiting on me
To love and cherish me the way you deny me
So here's to having the courage to leave

Forgiveness

Finding the words to say it
The feeling to mean it
The battle you fought to get there
Remember that it was always for you
Forgiveness is not about them
They may never deserve it
but you do
So forgive them for every tear you cried
For every time your heart ached
For every time you were left waiting
Or left feeling lonely and unloved
For every time you felt as if you weren't enough
Forgive them and heal
Love again and heal
Forgive them ...remember who you are and heal into greatness
Your best life awaits

Healing Comes in Time

You let go

I'm not resentful

I am sad that my efforts seemed in vain

But I am the one who had to change

The push pull wasn't working for me

You're coming and going as you please

Was hurting me

You living your best life...

Only stopping by when you needed the high of my love...

something genuine

The caress of my touch ...

me loving you too much

but it would never be enough

I cross your mind from time to time and

You seep in my thoughts unexpectedly

sometimes I smile

sometimes I want to cry both emotions are fine...

all healing comes in time

Why Can't You Love Me

Why can't you love me
I'm asking a question so just answer it
is my love oppressive or something you just can't get with
I'm tired of wondering I want to know
why can't you love me
haven't I done almost everything for you
loved you and adore you even more too even more too
you've been riding the fence it's at my expense
thinking about it now I'm wondering was it the dollars
because it sure don't make sense makes sense
why I keep going to bat for you
keeping your shit stacked for you
damn sometimes I feel trapped with you
and yet I stay for you
so why can't you
Why can't you let yourself be free to give me what I need
are you opposed to loving me
I mean I have been nothing but open heart it with you
Speaking my mind sharing my thoughts my dreams and motions
they say that a close mouth doesn't get feed
I heard what they said so I share with you all of me
from my toes to my head from my mind to my bed
and yet it angers me
the way you can come to me
but you can't love me
sometimes I think I should have been cold hearted with you
and maybe I wouldn't be dealing with this

believe it or not I am tired of the BS
sometimes I think that you are lost in translation
So why don't you face the facts
that only I can …only you can… only we can communicate on this level
only we can share this Passion
stimulate each other freely
break boundaries yes liberation revealed in the truth that there's power in our alliance
so why are you so scared to try it
sometimes you can be so in tune but only when you choose
tell me if that ain't being rude
you chant my thoughts and inhale my words
it's times I think that maybe you love my mind
do I need to repeat that because I wonder if you heard me the 1st time
I want you to love all of me from the way I cook
to the way sleep to the way my words form
to the way I sneeze from my attitude to the way I ride with you
love all of me and if I am something that you just can't handle
be strong enough to take a stand and say that too
I will not apologize for being me or for believing in what I see
for attempting to achieve what I believe will make me complete
I will not apologize for believing in that which we keep
are stronger are stronger than the secrets that used to be we
look me in my eyes and tell me can't you love me
The hardest thing in the world is to look in the mirror and love the reflection staring back at you yourself

I Know Love (Love Is….)

Today I realized.
I know love
And I have been in love
That I can give love
Somedays
Love is a train wreck waiting to happen
And I am laughing
Because i survived
Gave my all
Suffering thru the years
Crying thru the tears
Love didn't love me back
No love don't always love you back
Or won't always have my back
Today I am ok with that.
Because I know love
How to forget love
How to give love
Most of how to forgive love
Love is…
So many things
And it comes as quick as it goes
Stays and never leaves
Strong and weak
Bright as the sunshine
Dark with defeat

Love is…
Kindness and caring
Hoping and sharing
And yet it is bitter and mad
Disappointment and sad
Angry and still makes you laugh.
Love is…
Judged because it is not enough
Judge because it's too much
What if the love
Love gave was all love had
Would you still be mad
Feeling drained of your last
Love is…
Grateful to be around another day
Acknowledge the courage
It took to leave or stay
Because some days love is a train wreck waiting to happen
Love is…
Tragic in the last 5 minutes
Empowering from the beginning
Yes it is the same and different
Love hurts a lot but
Can heal each spot
Take you from the bottom
Drop you from the top
Love has no limits and yet

You are surrounded
Limitless but there are boundries
Today I realized i know love
That I have had love
That I have gave love
That i have forgiven love
For the tears that love has brought
Thankful for the lessons love has taught me
For the changes love has shown me
So if u asked me what love is
It is what ever you want it to be
Love is defined by what we believe

Affirmations

Affirmation 1

I am powerful

I am protected

I am smart

I am beautiful

I am intelligent

I am talented

I can do anything

I set my mind to

No one can stop me

Except for me

So I will get out of my way so I can great things

I am leader I will set good examples

I am somebody

I am already great

I am already great

I am already great

Yes I am

Affirmation 2

I honor myself

I deserve to be happy

Affirmation 3

I forgive myself
I deserve to be happy
I release all that no longer serves me
I love and accept myself

Affirmation 4

I love me
I am loved
I am surrounded by love
Love is in me
I am love

Affirmation 5

I expand my awareness
I am open to receive endless miracles daily

Affirmation 6

The new direction I am guided to follow will manifest miracles

Affirmation 7

I open the door to opportunity
I receive all that is for me

Affirmation 8

I call all my power back to me
On every level, realm and plane of existence
I choose to be the greatest version of myself
I am whole healthy and complete

Affirmation 9

I attract abundance and wealth with ease
I am fully supported in every way

Affirmation 10

Today I heal and release anything that has been standing in my way

Affirmation 11

I believe in me
I trust myself

I am growing in such an amazing way
I have created a safe place to bloom in
My truth is healing

Affirmation 12

I am safe to feel
I celebrate all of myself
I am connected mentally emotionally and spiritually
My heart is open to receive loving and healthy connections

Affirmation 13

I am a powerful creator

Affirmation 14

I release expectations and
I allow myself to flow into greatness

Affirmation 15

I am deserving of a fresh start

Affirmation 16

I am deserving of healthy relationships
I am receiving them now

Affirmation 17

I am walking in my Divine purpose

Affirmation 18

I am open to the flow and ease in my life

Affirmation 19

I honor my body and my mind

Affirmation 20

It is safe for me to be happy now
My happiness is beautiful

Affirmation 21

My Energy is sacred
I set and honor my boundaries clearly
I am worthy of all I desire
I release survival mode
I empower myself

Affirmation 22

I love myself and show up for myself
Fully and completely

Affirmation 23

I am Powerful beyond measure
I speak life love into myself and those I love

Affirmation 24

I love myself out loud
 I am resilient unstoppable amazing
limitless spirit
And that is a beautiful thing

Affirmation 25

What is for me will always find me

Affirmation 26

I only attract loving honest caring people and nourishing connections in my life

Affirmation 27

I am in a place where only love can reach me

Meditations

Release Meditation

Allow yourself to heal and have a breakthrough

Releasing the baggage means

Let that shit go

All of the memories of old that keep you holding to nothing

All things that made you feel fucked up.

All the crap you have played on repeat that sucked

The feelings of not enough

The fear, doubts and the worry

The anger and expectations

It's heavy let that shit go

The childhood trauma

The useless drama

The situation ships

The people who take and never give

Your Past and the tears cried

The trauma ties

The toxic lies

Let that shit go

Release that baggage that shiiit no longer serves you

Unapologetic Meditation

No apologies needed
For loving yourself
for standing your ground
For standing in your power
For taking time for myself
For your passion
For how deep you love

No apologies needed
For saying NO
for following my dreams
for loving someone

No apologies needed
For telling your truth
For ending unhealthy relationships

No apologies needed
For making yourself a priority
You are perfect imperfections
And you are your own kinda amazing yes you are magic
And there is no apology needed for that

Love Meditiation

Please don't drive or operate heavy machinery while listening to this Audio

Close your eyes… take a deep breath in through your nose 1 2 3, hold 123 and out through your mouth

Again

Inhaling all the love and light of the Universe 123 and hold 123 exhaling all doubt and fear

Now breathe normally

I want to relax all the muscles in your body

Starting with the top of head your face your jaw your ears

Release your tongue from the roof of your mouth

Relax the muscles in your neck, your shoulders your arms your chest your stomach your hips your thighs legs and your feet your toes

Good now

See the divine light coming through the top of your head touching and activating each chakra starting with your

Your crown third eye throat heart Solar plexus

Sacral root and anchoring into mother earth.

As you Listen to the sound of my voice

I want to know you are safe you are loved and

It's ok that you didn't realize it before now

Today and everyday forward you will remember and embrace all that you are

You are more than enough

You are amazing

You are fulfilled

You are resilient

You have purpose

It's ok that you didn't realize it before

Now

You only attracted what is for your highest good

Your peace is your

priority

Your energy is a gift

You will continue exist loudly

You are in a place where only love can reach you

Can you see it now

You are in a place where only love can reach you

Hear it now

You are in a place where only love can reach you

Yes feel it now

Feel that powerful vibration of love

its UNCONDITIONAL

Unapologetic

Genuine and it's for you

You are deserving of all this love

You are surrounded with that love

Embrace it all allow it to move through every cell in your body

You are loved

This love is yours to keep

You are in a place where only love can reach you

Now

As take your next breath

I want you to start to feel your body move your fingers and toes

And in your own time open your eyes

You are back in the room...enjoy your day or night

The Secret Meditation

The secret is you

Your love

Your energy

Your time

Your thoughts

Your emotions

Your laughter

Your light

Your joy

Your kindness

Your dedication

Your smile

Your Confidence

Your divinity

The secret is you

Powerful Person Meditation

You're never too old to re-write your story.

You can change your story...

You can change

Breathe trust yourself

now shift directions

Feel the energy flowing all around you

through you ... breathe

Hear the soundtrack to your life story changing songs as you grow

breathe

Flowing

Metamorphosis to liberation

Embracing each step

Breathe

Diving deep and release to harmony...yes

Planting and watering seeds of change for growth

Breathe

Shed all those yesterdays

Shed all those not enough

Shed those doubts fears

And

Allow your divine to shine through

Your kindness is powerful

Your smile is powerful

Your laughter is powerful

Your love is powerful

You are powerfully and wonderfully made of Love

Faith Meditation

So I seek ye that makes me whole

Found and hold my faith

Storms will come and go

But great spirit I will wait

Wait until you tell me to move

Share what you say share

Be there to do what you say do

Great spirit i thank you

For bringing me this far

For waking me this morning

I woke with song in my heart

I hear you when you say my blessings aren't far

Your love is fixed in my memory

Because of you I am a better me

I found peace within

Releasing the past

I now understand I am deserving of what I have

I understand the vision you gave me

Take the road less travelled

It matters

You reminded me that I matter

You told me to tell someone they matter

So my brothers my sisters my friends you matter

You will change someone's life today

Do the change continue to be great

Your voice your words, your kindness carries weight

Keep the faith

Get grounded today

You are loved you are needed and most importantly you are never alone

Roots Meditation

You are the roots to your tree

You have to nurture yourself

The water from your tears is cleansing

The sunshine from your smile

So smile often

Love from your hugs

Hugging yourself is powerful

If your life is out of order it is the roots that brings it back together

You are the roots

You are the one to make you happy

When you cry remember to breathe

Feel your feelings sit with them they are real

When you are in a dark place remember you are the light

Shine bright

You get mad remember how special you are inside

You are deserving of a good night sleep

Love yourself the way you want others too

Be free to be you

Take the time to learn things about yourself you never knew

Remember you are the glue

You can weather any storms in life

Any battle any fight

Tell yourself how much you love yourself tonight

And tomorrow and the day after that

Remember to have your own back

Standing up for your self is necessary

You are allowed to speak your truth

You can bring balance when you feel indifferent

Loves are you listening

Your love is a gift

It's timeless and binding

You are the roots to your tree

Only you can you make you complete

Remember who you are

When you open your eyes

You will feel your Divinity

Intense Day Shower Meditation

In this present moment, I want you to think of your relationship with water…

As it flows from your head to your feel

think of how it nourishes your body

cooling your core

Providing nutrients to your cells

restoring balance

Allow it to revitalize you

Releasing all of today

Any aches, any pain

Stress, discomfort

anger or sadness

All fear and doubt

See it washing all away

Feel the release

the lightness as it goes down the drain

and back to mother earth for transmutation.

Now take a deep breath

Inhale Love and light

Exhale gratitude

Enjoy your day or your night

Gratitude Shower Meditation

Water holds memory

Heals, restores

And amplifies vibration

So stand in gratitude

For water in all its abundance

As the water pours over you feel … all the good

Open your heart

Allow your joy to be amplified

Breathe and

Allow your peace to amplified

Speak life into yourself...

On others

Allow Your love to be amplified

There is no resistance just flow

flowing gracefully yes moving easily

Gently lovingly

Feel recharged

rejuvenated and restored

Now as this meditation ends and your day begins

Be thankful for the nourishment of the water

And it's many purposes

Take a breath inhaling love and light

Exhale in gratitude

Enjoy your day

Gratitude

Gratitude # 1

Gratitude, love,
Mindfulness, new beginnings
And grace

Gratitude # 2

Gratitude is remembering there is no redo
Just today
Being grateful for what is
Grateful for this moment
For every part of your journey
Remember that when you start making moves
To be positive be joyful
Be grateful
Most importantly be you
You are amazing

Gratitude # 3

I am so happy and grateful for the flow and ease in my life

Gratitude # 4

I am so happy and grateful for healthy communication

Gratitude # 5

I am so happy and grateful for my healthy body and mind

Gratitude # 6

I am so happy and grateful for the prosperity and abundance flowing into my life from unexpected and unlimited sources

Gratitude # 7

I am thankful for who I was yesterday and grateful for who I am today and the grace of who I am becoming

Gratitude # 8

I am grateful for all the
Love that surrounds me

Gratitude # 9

I am grateful for the well-lit and clear protected path

Gratitude # 10

I am grateful for the loving connections
And the overflowing support

Gratitude # 11

I am grateful the joy laughter and love in my life

Gratitude # 12

I am grateful for the balance

Gratitude # 13

I am grateful for the shift in my life
My healing is granted

Vibe Check

Vibe Check Puzzle

BHJHFCFBJNGOODKBHBVIBEOBELIANDCEKL
EXSQMOVEWHIKLFORGABNOLEGRATITUDEP
LEVOLVEHJUIBAGPPOINHITREKINDNESSLHL
ISAEINSPIREPODEASJUNPIBDGIVEMJUO[HEV
ENOUGHNOUFTVNUKLPCALMPESWWIKPSLO
VALUEBUTPOLOPDAWEELNESSKZWGHJIOME
EDISTANCEHOPHFDTRAVELLNNGKPOWEFUR
POWERFULGRDWACNNLOJJOYHOFSWGOODB
TUFSMKLYTTSMOTIVATIONJFDSWAPOSTAYL
FOCUSHTKPOBDSQQNJMAGNIFICENTIJOPRO
EMOTIONALHDPUTNFBJCONNECTLGPXZMAV
EHPLFRSFHLISTENFHIGTDHNFESACVNJOUE
LDEHKINDSDESIREKBVFPXZQAMOVEHMOPV
SELGHVSELFCAREPOSTIUNSTOPPABLEHOSC
WEALTHNKVFKONEBDJYTVXWAZSSKFHTEB
BOUNDRIESMPOCAREVKIGRATEFULNESSNM
MEDHYJLPAWXCCEDPROCESSGROWINGCHA
HEALINGGRANTEDFHIMKLPOSHIFTOPJNMM
NOITAITIDEMIMAGINEJOBRELEASEMKOPII
SUNSHINETFREABPITRUTHNOANGELFKBCM
GODDESSKIGFDSACUCLESACREDPEATVPOV
DIVINELYFGUIDEAGHJGOODBTAVEKEVARB
HONORJYDBYARPJYRFECNADNUBAERAUOY
UNIVERSEJMIFIMODSIWROSEQUARTZLOVE
EASEUFESCFBHNENERGYHHPOMHSHOLDW
SPACE HGMANIFESTHIPLKSBREATHEKPDL
GFDVKMLAUGHINGWAXZPORZNAUTRETOU
HCUOTRELAXATIONDONFCAPCVWALKING

Triumph

Dear My Sunray,

If you are reading this…

Congratulations on taking the journey to heal yourself! I am sure it was a lot, but you were and still are worth it.

By now you have set some boundaries and are still getting used to them. Stick to it. Remember to be gentle with yourself. All of this is a process. Some days you will feel like you are struggling but there will be plenty of victories.

Most importantly love on yourself daily. Let your love shine. You make the world a better place.

Thank you for that.

I'm sending you love light and hugs.

You are such a beautiful, amazing soul and you got this!

Happy living,
Shanie

About the Author

Shanie Ecole known by many names, Sunshine, Shanie the Artist, Shanie the poet and hails as "The Original Sunshine Princess of Poetry."

Her artistry has been featured on Yung-Ro's, The Counselor Album, Blacksnow's Just Tryna Live My Dreams Album, Gda Starr's The Break-up Album, numerous charitable events and expanded into her book "Telling Secrets Since Birth". Shanie hosted Snow Industries open mic shows at various venues but refusing to allow any to place her in a box she ventured into to the acting world and has been in plays such *as Karma, The Scarlet Letter, Millennium Women of Color and the Millicent Bradford Adoption Story as well as the movies: Love Is ... and Pipe Dreams.* Shanie started a line of note cards and paintings under the name of "You Are Poetry" as well as a plus sized line of shirts and purses called Poetically THICK. Shanie is a former spokesperson for March of Dimes, "Go Before You Show" and an internet radio personality on "\Grow Your Mind and Money" as well as "Shanie's Sunshine Lounge" which airs on old grumpyradio.com with her new show "The P word" due to air on Iconix Radio 2023.

She began journey as a healer a few years ago, not realizing it had begun long before she noticed it.

It has been nothing more rewarding and challenging (besides motherhood lol) but who doesn't love a good challenge? So, she started searching for her life's purpose and while on the way acquired several certifications as well as learning different energy healing modalities. She uses her divine intuition as well as her Angels, Dragons and Spirit guides to help her guide you on higher path. She is an Angelic Reiki Master, Dragon Energy Certified, Angel Oracle and Tarot Certified Card reader, Atlantean Healing

Practitioner, Angelic Mediumship Practitioner, Crystal Skull Guardian and Healing Granted is another beautiful piece to her journey.

A word from the author ...

Thank you for allowing me to share my gift of love with you.
Sending you love light and healing. REMEMBER You are loved and that's a beautiful thing.

www.ingramcontent.com/pod-product-compliance
Lightning Source LLC
Chambersburg PA
CBHW072335300426
44109CB00042B/1592